THE OCTOPUS'S GARDEN

THE SECRET WORLD UNDER THE SEA

black dog

by Dr. Mark Norman

First published 2008
This edition published 2009 by

black dog books

15 Gertrude Street
Fitzroy Vic 3065
Australia
61 + 3 + 9419 9406
61 + 3 + 9419 1214 (fax)
dog@bdb.com.au

Photo Credits — Roger Steene: pp 5, 8; Mark Strickland: p 23;
David Paul: pp i, 21. All other images: Mark Norman.

Designed by Guy Holt Illustration and Design.
Printed and Bound in China by Everbest Printing.

ISBN: 9781742030692

10 9 8 7 6 5 4 3 2 1

Contents

Wizards of the Sea

Octopuses and squid are like
the wizards of the sea. They are
brainy, can change shape and color,
disappear in a cloud of ink, throw away
their arms and grow new ones, and use
special potions and poisons.

Along with their relatives, the nautilus and cuttlefish, they live in all the oceans of the world, from the hot tropics to the cold deep sea. There are more than a thousand species, and they all have their own special tricks.

COCONUT OCTOPUS

The Coconut Octopus lives in areas of sand and mud where it is exposed to predators. It collects clam or coconut shells to use for protection.

It finds coconut shells, and can carry them around using its arms like stilts.

Sometimes it buries the shell halves under the sand, leaving a tiny slit to suck in water to breathe.

BLUE-RINGED OCTOPUS

The tiny Blue-ringed Octopus can fit into the palm of your hand. But its deadly venom is powerful enough to kill you.

The bright blue rings of these octopuses warn other sea creatures not to touch or attack.

MIMIC OCTOPUS

To scare away its predators, the Mimic Octopus changes shape to look like a poisonous animal. It can change from one form to another in the blink of an eye.

It can look like this banded sea snake by putting six arms down a hole and stretching out the other two arms.

It can look like a poisonous flatfish by spreading its arms around its body and gliding like a swimming fish.

SAND OCTOPUS

The Sand Octopus is an expert at hiding quickly. It makes its own quicksand by squirting fast jets of water to make the sand soft and loose. Then it dives in.

Once buried, the octopus uses its arms to make a chimney in the sand.

If attacked it makes the chimney collapse, staying buried until it is safe to emerge.

DAY OCTOPUS

The Day Octopus has an amazing ability to camouflage itself. To become invisible to its predators, it changes its shape and color, and can look like rock, coral or seaweed.

There is an octopus in this picture—can you see its eye and arms?

STRIPED PAJAMA SQUID

The Striped Pajama Squid is the size of a golf ball. Its striped skin warns fish that it tastes horrible. If attacked it squirts poison slime.

This squid swims by flapping its fins and flying through the water.

During the day it buries itself in the sand to hide.

GIANT CUTTLEFISH

Giant Cuttlefish have competitions to see who can make the best color changes. Their skin can change from black to white, or show moving zebra stripes.

They can also change shape to look like seaweed—can you see the cuttlefish in this picture?

BROADCLUB CUTTLEFISH

The Broadclub Cuttlefish can
use moving stripes to hypnotize
its prey, before shooting
high-speed tentacles
out to grab them.

If you show the cuttlefish a mirror, it will show off its stripes.

This cuttlefish can disguise itself by looking like a floating leaf.

CHAMBERED NAUTILUS

Nautiluses have been swimming in our oceans for millions of years. They bob around on the dark sides of coral reefs, sucking up hermit crabs.

Nautiluses swim around by squirting jets of water through their funnel.

ARGONAUT

Argonauts are octopuses that swim in the open ocean. If attacked they release an ink which can paralyze their predator's sense of smell.

The female argonaut makes a beautiful white shell, sometimes called a paper nautilus. She lays her eggs inside.

Argonauts can catch a ride from passing jellyfish.

Fact Files

Coconut Octopus (*Amphioctopus marginatus*)

The Coconut Octopus has a body about the size of a lemon. It feeds on shellfish that it catches in mud and sand. It will hide in anything, including clam shells, coconut shells and old tin cans. When angry, it puffs itself up and turns purple. It mainly hunts in the half light of dusk and dawn.

Distribution: Tropical Indian and west Pacific Oceans. Lives in depths of up to 590 ft.

Blue-ringed Octopuses (*Hapalochlaena* species)

There are at least 13 species of these small octopuses. Blue-ringed octopuses are some of the deadliest creatures in the world, and four species have been known to cause human deaths. Their saliva contains strong nerve poisons that they use to paralyze crabs. There is no known antidote to their venom.

Distribution: Australia to Japan. Lives in depths of up to 650 ft.

Mimic Octopus (*Thaumoctopus mimicus*)

This octopus lives on black sand plains in shallow waters, which are some of the most dangerous environments for a soft-bodied animal. It hunts during the day and has an amazing ability to change shape and color to look like other poisonous animals, such as banded sea-snakes, flatfish, lion fish, stingrays, or jellyfish. Scientists think that the octopus decides on which animal to mimic based on which predator is nearby.

Distribution: Papua New Guinea to the Red Sea. Lives in depths of up to 160 ft.

Sand Octopus (*Octopus kaurna*)

This octopus has a long, thin body about the size of a thumb. During the day it buries under the sand, and makes a chimney through the sand to the surface so it can suck in water to breathe. It uses slime to hold the chimney together. By night it hunts for crabs, shrimp, and worms.

Distribution: Southern Australia. Lives in depths of up to 160 ft.

Day Octopus
(*Octopus cyanea*)

This octopus has skin that can be raised as spikes to help it look like coral or weeds. It emerges at dawn and dusk to feed on lobsters, crabs and fish, and its home can be identified by the scattering of empty crab shells around the entrance. It can run along the sea floor using two of its arms like legs. This way it does not look like a regular octopus, so can slip past its predators.

Distribution: Indian and Pacific Oceans.
Lives in depths of up to 650 ft.

Striped Pajama Squid
(*Sepioloidea lineolata*)

This small squid looks like a golf ball with stripes. It hides buried in the sand during the day, and comes out at night to hunt shrimp, crabs, and fish. When buried, the little fingers of skin above its eyes stop sand falling into its gills. Its striped pattern warns fish that it is horrible to eat. If attacked, it squirts poisonous slime from glands under its body.

Distribution: Australia to Papua New Guinea.
Lives in depths of up to 820 ft.

Giant Cuttlefish
(*Sepia apama*)

Giant Cuttlefish males have long arms that look like flags. They stretch them out during color change competitions. They are the largest cuttlefish species in the world, and can grow up to three feet long. Like all cuttlefish, they have a white chalky cuttlebone inside their bodies that helps them float. Birds love eating and sharpening their beaks on cuttlebones.

Distribution: Australia.
Lives in depths of up to 330 ft.

Broadclub Cuttlefish
(*Sepia latimanus*)

This cuttlefish is amazing at color changes. It hunts by slowly swimming towards small shrimp and fish, while flashing zebra stripes up and down its arms —almost hypnotizing its prey before shooting high-speed tentacles out to grab them. It can hide from attackers by changing shape to look like a mangrove leaf. If shown a mirror, males will fight their reflection.

Distribution: Australia to Fiji and Japan.
Lives in depths of up to 160 ft.

Fact Files

Chambered Nautilus (*Nautilus* species)

These types of animals have been swimming in our oceans for 500 million years. Once, they reached 10 feet in diameter, and swam around sucking up trilobites and shellfish. Today only six small species exist, hiding on the deep, dark sides of coral reefs. They rise at night to hunt hermit crabs and eat dead animals.

Distribution: Tropical Indo-Pacific.
Lives in depths from 160 ft to 2100 ft.

Argonaut (*Argonauta* species)

Also called paper nautiluses, these octopuses spend their lives swimming around in the blue water of the open ocean, never touching the sea floor. The females can grow up to 12 inches long, and make beautiful thin white shells in which to lay their eggs. If threatened, they will use the spikes on their shell to ram predators in the nose. The males are less than an inch long and have no shells.

Distribution: Tropical and cool oceans around the world.
Lives in depths of up to 650 ft.

Dr. Mark Norman is a research scientist with Museum Victoria. He has dived in oceans all around the world, and studies octopuses, nautiluses, squid and cuttlefish.

For more information go to:

ABRS Species Bank site:
www.environment.gov.au/biodiversity/abrs/online-resources/species-bank

Tree of Life website:
www.tolweb.org/Cephalopoda

ArgoSearch website:
www.argosearch.org.au

Norman, M.D. 2000. *Cephalopods: a world guide.* IKAN Publishing, Frankfurt.

Norman, M.D. and Reid, A. 2000. *A guide to squid, cuttlefish and octopuses of Australasia.* CSIRO and Gould League of Victoria, Melbourne.